Tiers
Of Growth

Rahma Gabdon

Tiers of Growth

Contents

Dedication

It was narrated from the prophet Muhammad (peace and blessings be upon him) that,

"He who does not thank people (for their favors) has not thanked Allah."

Ahmad and Al-Bukhari in Al-'Adab Al-Mufrad. Thus, I would like to take this section to express gratitude and thanks to the following. Firstly, I would like to give thanks to my Lord for granting me the brain capacity, strength, aid, time, provisions, sustenance, blessings, and numerous other virtues that He has showered upon me that without them nothing would be possible.

Secondly, those individuals whom He has made a means for me to complete this. My parents, thank you for always loving me and believing in me (especially when I didn't believe in myself). My mother Nura, my mother, my mother. To whom I would not be who I am today without her strength and continuous support. No words can repay anything you have done for me nor could I ever repay you with mere actions even if I gave you the world and all it contains. Thank you Hooyo. To my beloved children. Thank you and sorry for all the times Mummy was prized away from you be it in spirit or in person.

Thank you to my friends for everything that you have helped and shared with me. I always left our talks feeling inspired, motivated, passionate and full of thoughts surrounding this book. You inspired me to carry this until the end, I could not have asked for a better group of friends. Thank you, to all my friends who have given me respite during the stressful times by providing me with well needed laughs in between. You are dearly appreciated and held in high esteem by me. To my friends who have listened to me relentlessly talk about or share my writings, thank you deeply.

Lastly, I would like to pay special mention to those near and far who made the choice to read my small collection of writings. To those silent readers whom I do not get the chance to hear from. To those who contact me and give me valuable feedback. Thank you all for taking the time out of your lives to read my work and support my small muses. Thank you to those that have inspired me in any way and who motivate me to work on my passion. I pray this brings a benefit to your lives in some way.

This has been an unbelievable rollercoaster, and it began with a dream, as all great journeys should.

Rahma Gabdon

September 2021, London.

Introduction

begin with beseeching the name of Allah the most Merciful the oft Forgiving. I elieve every person has a story, every story has a purpose, every purpose must be ulfilled. Oftentimes, your struggle may become somebody's handbook for survival. The purpose of this book is to aid my sisters in faith. Truly, something beautiful can rise out of a place of pain. The only direction from hitting a low point is upwards. Oftentimes, that place of pain prepared you for bigger and better things. Although hen you are in that place of pain it is hard to see beyond it. Allah promises eases rith hardship. It is his Lordly promise. Feel what you need to feel and then let it go ut never let it consume you. You may have felt stuck and unsure of what was ahead, ave full faith that Allah will gear your life in the most perfect way. Such that you rill look back at the life you left behind as a new woman. Finally saving herself. inally doing it without anybody. Nobody able to recognize her because she doesn't eed them anymore. This new woman is you and I and I must say that it looks eautiful on you!

Empowerment

Allah is with you. When it comes to your journey, He is with you. This should bring about great ease and comfort to an individual. Allah is all aware. As can be seen in the story of prophet Yusuf alayhi salaam. Allah wants to always make clear to his believers that He does not forget who is doing what for you, to you, or even against you. Subsequently, what you are doing against or for others. He does not forget. Allah is all aware. The eyes of those that oppress may sleep but sleep does not overcome Allah. Allah will solve trials and tribulations in this life. He hastens for the resolution as a means of comfort for the oppressed. Even if it takes forty years.

In the story of prophet Yusuf alayhi salaam as mentioned by

Shaykh 'Abd ur-Rahman ibn Nasir as-Si'di Lessons Learnt From The Story Of Yusuf it mentions,

As such, it contains various signs and lessons for anyone who asks for them and seeks guidance and integrity. This is due to what it contains of one evolving circumstance to another; from one ordeal to another; from facing challenges to being blessed; from humiliation and slavery to honour and authority; from division to unity and fulfilled aspirations; from grief to joy; from abundance to scarcity, from scarcity to abundance,

4

from famine to plenitude and from hardship to ease, amongst the other things this great story embodies.

This story includes countless amazing benefits. It shows various journeys transferring from one situation to another. Whoever realises that after hardship and trials there comes about goodness and blessings will be granted peace of mind. It is a glad tiding to those who take heed. Allah will never aid the oppressor. Allah is the One who is ever watchful over your intentions and thus He will keep you steadfast upon it. Whomsoever withholds the rights of others is an oppressor and for Him there is no helper that will stop him from the punishment of Allah. In the tafsir of Sheikh Abdurahman Nasir Si'di he said,

"nobody from the creation will benefit him or help him".

There are many themes in the story of Prophet Yusuf alayhi salaam. One message that is reoccurring is not to grieve, Allah will give you victory even if it is after a time. Allah is testing you and building you for bigger and better. This is his Lordly promise. There are stark warnings to those doing wrong to those who have nobody except Allah. Do not try to test Allah. By Allah if everybody knew that Allah would repay the oppressor and he was certain of this, he would not oppress others.

It is narrated on the authority of Abu Umama that the Messenger of Allah (may peace be upon him) observed: He who appropriated the right of a Muslim by (swearing a false) oath, Allah would make Hell-fire necessary for him and would declare Paradise forbidden for him. A person said to him: Messenger of Allah, even if it is something insignificant? He (the Holy Prophet) replied:(Yes) even if it is the twig of the arak tree

Sahih Muslim.

This is a great hadith and shows a severe warning to those who oppress even if it may be something small. The twig of this specific tree is more commonly known as where the miswak is taken from. A miswak is considered something small and weak so much so that it can be snapped in half easily. If you are amongst those who have taken the rights of others unjustly by Allah, you will not live a life of happiness.

5

Purify yourself from the rights of others before death reaches you. Otherwise, it will become a punishment for you in this life and hereafter. Just look at the punishment for this oppression and taking the rights of others unjustly. Even if the oppressed is a disbeliever and makes supplication, Allah will accept his duah. This is not for a like for the disbelief but a love for justice. A Just Lord.

It was narrated from Abu Hurairah that the Messenger of Allah (ﷺ) said:

> *There are three whose supplications are not turned back: A just ruler, and a fasting person until he breaks his fast. And, the supplication of one who has been wronged is raised by Allah up to the clouds on the Day of Resurrection, and the gates of heaven are opened for it, and Allah says, 'By My Might I will help you (against the wrongdoer) even if it is after a while'.*

Abu Hurairah from Sunan Ibn Majah.

The Prophet, peace and blessings be upon him, also said,

> *"Every consequence of sin is delayed by Allah, as he wills, until the Day of Resurrection, except for injustice, disobedience to parents, or severing family ties. He will hasten the punishment of those who commit them in this world before he dies."*

Al-Adab al-Mufrad, Sahih (authentic) according to Al-Albani.

If the world becomes narrow on you turn to Allah and do not pay attention to those who harm you. You are the highest-ranking person in your life so ultimately you make the decisions. You get to evict whomsoever you want along with their toxicity. In the worst of moments Allah plans the best of plans, guides, and unravels the best of lessons for us. So have certainty therein and flow and execute according to those plans. Prophet Yusuf alayhi salaam was left for dead in the well by the very people who were supposed to protect and support him. It may be that those closest to you cause you the most pain and harm. But you must not lose hope, Allah will always aid the oppressed. Everything Allah does is with a Lordly wisdom. However, we are unaware of the wisdom behind it although sometimes we may be shown a glimpse of what Allah has saved you from when it has passed. What was next for Yusuf alayhi salaam was that a passer-by found and sold him as a slave. This eemingly went from bad to worse although he was from the best of mankind. He was instantly sold as a slave being devastating. Despite this, prophet Yusuf had a firm sense of empowerment and strong faith in His plan which enabled him despite the predicament he was put in. These characteristics kept him strong and stable which led to him empowering himself and others when things around him were going outwardly wrong. Anyone that has been wronged can reach this conclusion without a second thought especially where it is clear-cut. This means that the realities and truth is always revealed.

It does not matter how powerful or authoritarive the oppressors are. Sooner or later the truth comes out. It does not matter how deceptive and manipulative they are. Nor how sweet or sharp their tongue is in terms of deflection and attempts to conceal the truth. Sooner or later Allah will reveal all of it. Even if He brings forth miracles to aid you. It will happen. Fundamentally, Islam warns every human and most importantly every Muslim so that they do not wrong or oppress others. Allah will take you into account just as they will be held accountable. No stone will be left unturned on that day. It does not matter how charming their character may appear and how much of a position they may have, it will not be left alone in the slightest. Allah will give glad tidings in many forms to aid and support the oppressed.

Allah inherently empowers the believers who embody goodness. He facilitated it for it to be established. Whatever good that you have in you if you try to implement with those nearest to you Allah will empower it. Regardless of how you were low and belittled to begin with. You must have that certainty that this is the reality of Allah. He will not see good in your heart and leave it. He will place an inundation of blessings therein. Plans of Allah are always for empowerment even though you may have a dark cloud of sadness engulfing you at the time. Allah will deliver you from his sadness. Seek deliverance from Him. His plan is to empower you and to empower others. The weaker a person is, the more that Allah empowers and takes care of him. Allah will play His role in accordance to assist you. This is not an abstract empowerment it is a physical means Allah will send you. He will send you aid and help from sources you cannot decipher. It is His promise if you come with fear of Allah. This alone will give you the better plan. Allah's plan.

And whoever puts his trust on Allah, sufficient is Allah for him".

Surah Al-Talaq: Verse 3.

Put your faith in Allah and practise tawakkul in Him. This means that your heart is connected to Him and that you await and hope all good from Allah alone. This is the epitome of servitude and tawheed. Simultaneously, you rely on Allah to deflect all harm from you. Your heart must have firm conviction and hope in Him a thousand times over. You must personify the belief that Allah is sufficient for you. From the great names of Allah is the name of Al-Kaafi. If you internalise this, it allows an individual to be free from expecting anything from mankind and he will hand all His affairs to Allah. You will be an individual who will be entirely independent of all besides Allah. This is the essence of worship to Allah. It is said that the Salaf would ask Allah for everything even that which is as small as their daily salt.

There is a narration of a young boy who believed in Allah in the lengthy hadith which can be found in Sahih Muslim. This young slave of Allah firmly embodied this when the King during his era claimed to be a Lord. The young boy refused to follow his blasphemy, so he ordered for him to be killed, by throwing him off the highest point if he refused to denounce his faith. He recited the duah asking Allah to suffice him from their plans. The mountains moved and all the people sent to harm him fell off. He returned to the King unscathed, and it was then ordered for him to be taken to the middle of the ocean and thrown in. The young boy recited the same duah and the men died in the middle of the ocean whilst he returned once again walking to the King. Unscathed. This was to the dismay of the King. What would you expect from a person who beseeched Allah with His name Al-Kaafi? Allah in turn sufficed him from their harm. By Allah you do not worry about a thing and place it in front of Allah except that He will suffice you completely.

Ali ibn Abi Talib reported: The Messenger of Allah, peace and blessings be upon him, said,

"O Allah, suffice me with your allowances against your prohibitions, and make me independent of all those besides you."

8

The prophet Muhammad pbuh came with complete submission and perfection in his faith in Allah. The believer must come with the means and put his faith and heart in Allah. You must not become confident in your limited ability. The name of Allah Al-Kaafi also teaches us that the believers were put through difficulties and tests during the time of the prophet, but Allah saved them from the plotting of the enemies. At times they were put in a corner whereby no help was visible. Allah illustrates us this in various places in the Quran and hadith. In the battle of Badr Allah sent down thousands of angels to aid them as an army in their defence. When they were put into a difficult situation this is how Allah protected and defended them from the enemy. Allah will never forsake His promise and His might is with you. But it is your faith and certainty in Him that is weak.

This world is run by Allah's order thus the plotting of the people is weak because everything ultimately falls under His command. The fire did not burn Ibrahim alayhi salaam rather it was cooled by Allah. The whale did not harm Yunus alayhi salaam. The same ocean that swallowed Pharoah and his army Musa alayhi salaam walked upon it unharmed. Thus, the plotting and plans of the enemy is feeble so hand over your faith and affairs completely in Allah. Stand up during the late hours of the night with humility to Him and beg Him to rectify all your affairs. Allah is enough for you and will suffice you. The believer's ammunition that he fights with is duah so do not arrive empty handed to the battleground.

Another theme that can be seen in Surah Yusuf is that Allah is the best protector. Al Wali. The brothers of Yusuf alayhi salaam plotted against him despite being his immediate family. Sadly, it may be that the person you would take a bullet for is the one behind the gun. No matter who they are and how it looks on the outside, Allah is ultimately the best protector like no other. From the wisdom of Allah is that every sin committed Allah delays the result until the day of judgement whereby He forgives or punishes them as He wishes. Except for the oppression of His servants, this one is never delayed. Allah mandated on Himself that he will give the oppressed respite before the oppressor's death. Perhaps by a way of an affliction, a test, his honour, his wealth, or an evil ending. The oppressor is repaid in a myriad of ways. What is

9

important is that Allah will recompense him. Allah is a Just Lord, He created us and provided for us, yet He forbade oppression on Himself. So who are you to oppress?

Abu Huraira reported: The Messenger of Allah, peace and blessings be upon him, said,

> *"Whoever wrongs his brother in his honour or anything else should resolve the matter today before it cannot be resolved with gold and silver coins. If he has good deeds to his credit, they will be taken from him according to the measure of his injustice. If he has no good deeds left, he will bear the evil deeds of the one he has oppressed."*

Ṣaḥīḥ al-Bukhari.

Spiritual Murder

One of the biggest trials for mankind is self-admiration and the ego which makes one transgress and forget his Lord. The term *narcissism* came from the ancient Greek myth of Narcissus, a beautiful young boy who rejects the love of others as unworthy, until he comes across what he thinks is the greatest beauty so much that he falls in love - but it is to his own reflection in water. The longer he stares at his image, the more he is driven by both passion and heartache, and over time he dies in this state of despair. A fit ending for a narcissist if you ask me.

Pathological narcissism has long held an important hold on the imagination throughout history. Mythological, biblical and other religious writings and doctrines have included sanctions against vanity, and the dangers of choosing self-love over the love of others and society. These dangers, long discussed in stories, paintings and plays, have found a modern form in the presentation of a particular kind of personality style, narcissistic personality disorder...

Grenyer, Brin. (2013). Historical overview of pathological narcissism.

In essence narcissistic personality disorder or more commonly known as NPD is a mental condition whereby a person has an increased sense of self-importance and an excessive urge for admiration. Narcissism is a spectrum disorder which means that it exists on a scale ranging from those with a few characteristics of it to those who are fully fledged narcissist. They are more concerned with how they look then what they feel. Hence, superficial charm is one of the top criteria for people with this disorder. They appear to be good people on the outside and many do not believe their victims. It is the pursuit of gratification by the ego. In other words, it is all about them getting what they want, how they want it and when they want it.

In these Greek myths there are many things mentioned that are contrary to our religion and our Islamic morals. Our religion has placed severe warnings against vanity and the dangers of choosing the ego. Allah tells us the dangers of having a seeds worth of pride and that it can cause one not to enter paradise. The prophet mentioned that we should love the prophet more than ourselves which cuts the ego. As is shown in the hadith Abdullah ibn Hisham reported:

We were with the Messenger of Allah, peace and blessings be upon him, and he was holding the hand of Umar ibn al-Khattab. Umar said to him, "O Messenger of Allah, you are more beloved to me than everything but myself." The Prophet said, "No, by the one in whose hand is my soul, until I am more beloved to you than yourself." Umar said, "Indeed, I swear by Allah that you are more beloved to me now than myself." The Prophet said, "Now you are right, O Umar."

Ṣaḥīḥ al-Bukhari.

The Arabic term for a narcissist is 'anaani' which comes from the pronoun used for the self. Meaning, me, myself, and I. This was the very reason why Ibless refused Allah's order to bow down to Adam. When he was asked what prevented him from prostrating his response was that he was better than him because he was created from fire as opposed to Adam being created from clay. In this instance Iblees planted the first seed of arrogance and ego into Allah's creation, which many of mankind would follow suit. An example of a grandiose narcissist in the Quran can be illustrated by the story of Pharoah. He was so self-absorbed and self-obsessed that he went far as to claim to be Allah, and that there was no Lord besides him. What greater blasphemy is there?

Here is a list of what narcissists usually do to their targets :

- Insults their target very often. Then lie when confronted about it, or say it was a joke, this is called gaslighting.

- When confronted with their behaviour, they pretend to be innocent and play the victim. Everything is always your fault, even when it's obviously not.

- They always have a justification for every bad thing they do. They think they are always right.

- Very controlling, they tell you how to live, but they can live any way they want. Very hypocritical. They accuse you of what they're doing to you this is called projection.

- Portraying themselves as angels outside, when they are demons with their family and especially their target.

- They need to be constantly praised and looked up to and never can be left alone.

- They want you to fail while pretending to want you to succeed (they can be very convincing, after all they are good actors).

- They never say they are sorry for hurting you, and if they do it is with an agenda and again it is your fault.

- They will poison your favourite activities; they do not want you to be happy or to get pleasure. This stems from the emptiness they feel inside. They also poison other useful activities like important skills which will help you in the future. They do not want you to have skills, they want you to be as weak as possible.

- When you want to leave the relationship with a narcissist, they beg you to stay with them and cry crocodile tears. They may even fake an illness or threaten to self-harm. They are the best actors. - Sometimes nice, sometimes cruel. You never know where you stand with them.

- You will be forever walking on eggshells.

- They pretend to be "victims", and they blame the target for their own behaviour.

- They are incredibly arrogant and sadistic. They see the target as weak, and deserving to suffer. They think they are models to be followed.

- Like Pharoah some think they are like God-like. The attributes ascribed to Allah alone. All-powerful, all-knowing, whatever the sick fantasy they live in.

- A 'religious' narcissist will even try to change the meaning of scriptures to suit their needs. Superficial charm so much that everyone surrounding them thinks they are nice and everything good under the sun, but behind closed doors that illusion they sold you soon goes away.

- They have a past of chaos and destruction but again it is never their fault.

Narcissists are psychologically incapable of taking the blame. Unless it serves them a purpose. If you must hurt other people to feel powerful, you are an extremely weak individual. Stop expecting honesty from people who live a daily lie. They are spiritually dead which explains why they seek to spiritually murder others, contrary to them loudly professing religion. They cannot withstand an emotional connection or love. They never loved you and never will, they only use and abuse people. It is a total scam and the biggest one at that. They always have a motive. They are very specific in their reason for being in a relationship and it does not fit the universal need we all desire which is to love and be loved. If you have something they want, and you are vulnerable they will harvest you for your resources. Sadly, you will be the last one to find out. Deliberately trying to strip you is part of their natural method.

"A man who lies to himself, and believes his own lies, becomes unable to recognize truth, either in himself or in anyone else, and he ends up losing respect for himself and for others. When he has no respect for anyone, he can no longer love, and in him, he yields to his impulses, indulges in the lowest form of pleasure, and behaves in the end

like an animal in satisfying his vices. And it all comes from lying — to others and to yourself."

Fyodor Dostoyevsky.

There are people in the world for whom the lights are on, but no one is home. That is a powerful imagery because you see, they never come home. They spend majority of their time running away from reality. In essence they are running from a huge void inside, they are running away from the reflection in the mirror and the permanent inner deadness. They are running away from something they will never escape. The real self.

Do not be tricked into thinking they are unaware of the abuse; narcissistic people know what they are doing. It is like a mask they put on when and with whom it suits. There is so far you can go carrying a face that does not belong to you. Until the mask falls and eventually the real ugly face will be shown. This mask they carry not only hides their real self from the world they also use it to hide from themselves. Narcissistic people possess a worrying number of hypocritical characteristics. Some say whenever a narcissist opens his mouth it is always followed by a lie. Lying is something that comes secondary to a narcissist, their entire life after all is a web of fabrications they have created.

Narrated 'Abdullah bin 'Amr: The Prophet (☐) said, "Whoever has the following four (characteristics) will be a pure hypocrite and whoever has one of the following four characteristics will have one characteristic of hypocrisy unless and until he gives it up.

1. Whenever he is entrusted, he betrays.

2. Whenever he speaks, he tells a lie.

3. Whenever he makes a covenant, he proves treacherous.

4. Whenever he quarrels, he behaves in a very imprudent, evil and insulting manner.

Ṣaḥīḥ al-Bukhari.

They oftentimes cover their wrongs by eloquent speech, diverting, blaming others and self-interest. They have a greater interest with themselves and this one has no boundaries and can lead to the destruction of nations. They have this selfishness because they feel entitled. Entitled to people's time, money, energy, and anything else they may want. If prophet Yusuf alayhi salaam fought back with his brothers, they may have killed him, but he did not react aggressively even to defend himself. He accepted the decree of Allah that He would always save Him. Allah gave him glad tidings of this in the form of a dream. He had certainty in Allah's plan.

Narcissists love to play the victim, and this helps energise the flying monkeys and smear campaign against you. People are more likely to sympathise attacks when it seems to be defensive. Essentially, playing the victim gets them exactly what they crave, constant attention, adoration, and sympathy for how they suffered. Without this the narcissist finds themselves in a terrifying situation, they must come face to face with their self-loathing core persona. Ignore them because what you feed will grow. Anybody who wants to believe their nonsense is unimportant in your life journey. After all this is your life journey, do not waste it on those who do not deserve access to you. The narcissists veil and the layers of deception it comes with, will slip at some point. Until then get on with your life and be happy. You will not lose real friends, you will not lose real relationships when you start standing up for yourself. But what you do get rid of are abusers, manipulators, and control freaks who seek to destroy you. They will be too busy finding faults in you while you were too busy overlooking all of theirs.

The narcissist is your worst enemy disguised at first as your helper. Dark disguised as light. Hate disguised as love. Predator disguised as friend. Lies disguised as truth. Betrayal disguised as loyalty. Evil disguised as good. Apathy disguised as empathy. Taker disguised as giver. Abuse disguised as affection.

And one day, just like that the whole game changed. No one is coming from the stars to light your darkness. They did not kill you all they did was make you better so you can perfectly arrive at your destiny and perfectly pursue your Lord given purpose. Some events in your life come to sharpen your vision so look a little deeper to see beyond the surface. Seek your victory for your ultimate clap back. Be the light or yourself. Perhaps a person with high status next to the people is meaningless and owly next to Allah. Perhaps a person with a low status next to the people is high nd lofty with Allah. Do not treat the symptoms, treat the cause. Do not accept the crumbs. Bake an entirely new cake and enjoy it while you are at it.

Practise and embody defiant self-love and know in the city of your soul what your ue value is and what you bring to the table. Stay in your place of peace not in pieces nd move on with your life. The time Allah has given you is too precious to stay and atch dysfunction for nothing but more dysfunction. Do not let anyone break you nd come back like it is okay. It is not! You are not to be used whenever its onvenient. Life is too short to waste on game players. O person beware of the erson who wants to act like nothing ever happened and will deflect and place the lame on you. You must know your worth. When you really know it, you will walk little differently. Do not go back to that which broke you. Take care of your heart, ne most precious thing you own.

Narcissists are being used by shaytaan to try and destroy Allah's people. Most of ou have been abused beyond limits, character assassination, deep rooted emotional, nental, and physical pain. I want you who is reading this to understand that Allah w everything you went through. The narcissist may believe they got away with alculated evil. They will do what they do best, act as if they never did any wrong nd you are the problem. You must be strong and encourage yourself daily with llah's aid. Your destiny is secured in the name of Allah. They will do everything ossible for you to fail, but Allah does everything for you to rise above. Allah has a aping and sowing system that the narcissist cannot and will not escape. Everything as a beginning and an end except Allah. Try not to stress yourself but rather count our blessings. A lot of people have no awareness about narcissistic abuse or nderstand what is happening. If you stay long enough, they will make you go insane. et your boundaries and protect your energy. They come to steal and destroy. Allah ame to give us life in abundance. Things get better with time.

A psychologically numbing, demeaning, invalidating, dehumanising *addictionship* is hat it is. They often spend most of the time abusing you and the remaining trying convince you they are not abusive. That the problem lies with you changing everything to try to please them, of course something which can never be reached. If you ever find yourself feeling anxious, confused, and worthless there is a reason for it. Trust yourself, you are not crazy, and you are not imagining it. Your body is trying to tell you something. Everything you see about them is nothing more than an illusion, they will lie, cheat, steal and abuse. They will drain you emotionally and commit all type of chaos without a care in the world. But if anything is done to them, they cannot handle it, victim mentality at its essence. Bottom line is to never trust a narcissist, they are not honest and lack any type of principles.

They may try to vilify you but hang in there and keep on working on your passion. Allah will open the entire world for you all you have to do is keep doing the good. Goodness always wins, evil will never win. Evil goes against the commands of Allah. Do not focus your energy on trifling people who believe they are hurting you but eventually only shoot themselves in the foot. Love yourself, love the life Allah gave you and all the blessings therein. I know initially it will be hard but that is how this world is supposed to be. But you got this, you got this.

Some of us have been through things so traumatic that the human mind cannot comprehend it. Yet we fight and persevere every single day and night. If that is not strength, I do not know what is. You are a survivor. The journey to healing is not easy but it is very rewarding once you have reached the fruitful destination. You must realise that you were trying to help the very person who wanted you to drown. You cannot fix someone who does not want to be fixed nor do they acknowledge the problem in the first place. But you can and you will lose yourself in the process of doing so. Guess what, the movie ends, and you win because you are free of them.

I love the saying that you can be lonely with or without people but the loneliest is being around the wrong people. Remove the voices that bring more toxicity to your surroundings. When your mental health is being disrespected and destroyed you are literally dying a slow torturous death. Never become so thirsty that you drink from every cup presented to you, that is how you get poisoned. Get out and love yourself first. Life is short. Love yourself and take care of yourself. No one is coming to save you, to validate you or to give you permission. This has always been your job. You must love yourself ever so **ferociously** to rebuild yourself.

No amount of sleep is enough when it is your soul that is tired. They did not care they never did. It was never about you. It was about them, trying to feel human and be as good a person as you. They will never manage to do that. It is not in their nature. They treat other people this way, you were not their first and you will certainly not be their last.

If you do not heal from that which hurt you, you will bleed on those that did not stab you. Moving on from certain experiences must have progression. You must not be stuck in the emotion; you must trust yourself. It takes you trusting yourself and having full certainty in Allah to be able to get to that point or you will be forever stuck and bitter. One loss does not equal forever, oftentimes that one loss proves to be a huge gain. Your own mind frame can be toxic and not a good sign of recovery or healing.

Heal so you can hear what is being said without the filter of your wound. It can oftentimes lead to your own toxicity which can rub off on others. Many people become bitter and sometimes neurotic off these negative experiences, and they will blame everyone around them leading them to become a professional victim. Being stuck in this mode looking for soothing from others. Staying stuck in a position that will not help you will only cripple you. At some point you must move on and graduate you cannot be forever stagnant. Rebuild the trust you lost in yourself. Remember who you were before they tried to convince you that you were worthless.

The victory of Allah comes with the smallest of means to provide glad tidings to the oppressed. Allah will test the oppressor from exactly where he oppressed from, he will drink from the same cup he served others. In the story of Maryam alayhi salaam Allah gave her glad tidings of a son that she will have without a father. People accused her of that which she was free from to the extent she fled in fear from her home. Allah gave her a son who was a prophet and spoke in infancy to free his mother from what they accused her of. Allah granted her ease through the very thing which caused her worry and anguish that she wished she had not been born. Allah exemplifies to His servants His ability, the might of His authority and that He has power over all things. Allah will empower the oppressed, this is His promise which has no deadline and never loses an address.

The longer the wait the sweeter the promise of Allah is. Perhaps his own oppression is faster against him then your supplication. At the time Allah wills not when you demand it. Thus, you must beautify yourself with purification and keeping steadfast in waiting, until the believer sees how Allah repays the oppressor. Oppression and transgression are amongst the things which Allah shows its outcome in this life and the punishment of Allah is severe.

Samarqandi reported: Sufyan al-Thawri, may Allah have mercy on him, said,

> *"For you to meet Allah Almighty with seventy sins between you and Allah would be easier on you than to meet him with a single sin between you and his servants."*

Tanbīh al-Ghāfilīn.

These following steps can help overcome people who have suffered narcissistic abuse.

1. Acknowledgement: Recognise that wrong is being done to you, abuse is abuse even if it is not physical. Some men will feel proud and boast that they have never laid hands on a woman, but their loophole is breaking women's spirits with a myriad of abuse and calling themselves kings for being different. A common trait is that they do not want you to heal hence why they keep you entrapped in the cycle of abuse. They do not want you to have clarity and want to keep you trauma bonded so as to cloud your vision. Within clarity, there is healing so take your time and heal.

2. Defence: Train and discipline yourself not to cause more harm either to yourself or the perpetrator especially when we are vulnerable and weak. This one is especially important as victims of this type of abuse are prone to picking up defensive ways to protect themselves. This is called reactive abuse and is a coping mechanism but now you must forgive yourself and move forward. When you have the chance to cause harm the boundary is that you do not oppress.

3. Connection: You must have a bond and strong connection with Allah. You cannot ultimately win if a bond with Him is absent. Ultimately what matters is your relationship with Him.

4. Healing: If you have been abused you must take some time out to heal. Everything moves in its own way and is set by the decree of Allah. We cannot reach certain milestones before others so take it easy because healing is a deep and timely process. You must practise some serious self-accountability, what was missing within you? What did you lose? You are hurting because you stopped loving you. Cutting ties with people who consistently hurt you is not enough; you must also cut ties with the version of you who allowed it to continue for as long as it did. This is not to be minimize the tremendous abuse caused onto you. But you must grieve them as if they have died because quite frankly the person you knew never existed. It is ok to mourn the individual you were sold to believe they were. Do not be heartbroken over a love that did not even exist.

Ultimately, you must be strong and the greatest power you have in your hands is ur soul. Constantly seek the help of Allah and His aid will shower down on you. is incumbent on us to realise that most people on this earth are traumatised by a ies of events in childhood or adulthood. Even as an adult part of your innocence n still be stolen, something narcissists do quite naturally because they are so deeply arred themselves. Take the time and educate yourself and you will soon realise you e not alone. There are numerous help groups and thousands of victims speaking t about this disease. Sadly, some stay for a lifetime before realising there is a name r these people. They greatly lack any ability to empathise with others. It is the ight of arrogance when a person decides that you need to be controlled and anipulated. Covert narcissists are in essence sheep in public and wolf at home. ey would rather impress a stranger and go above and beyond then take care of eir own family. Living an entire life to please the people and seek praise and a me. You are a pawn in a game that you never wanted to play, and you are going want out. The narcissist does not want to heal nor for you to heal, but your body eps count.

Trauma is not all in your head. It is also in your heart, body, nervous system, and deep in the crevice your soul. Look at it this way. It was not only your mind that went through the experience rather it was every fibre of you. Narcissistic abuse is insidious, imagine it as something that sneaks up on you and before you know it you are helplessly trying to climb out of a pit of despair that you had no idea you had even fallen into. Consequently, your body keeps score of it even if your mind tries to rationalise and deny it your body starts to fall apart. Forgive yourself. Try to love yourself a little more on the hard days. When the heart is at peace the body shows it. Remember to them you are merely an appliance, no different to an oven or fridge. At most they will miss the service you provided them but never miss you, you are easily replaceable. Everybody to them is replaceable.

Your hereafter

ake care of your hereafter and Allah will take care of the rest. One of the Salaf ould say, I become happy if I ask Allah and He answers, but I have a greater ppiness if I ask Allah and He delays it. The choice is in His control we must believe at He is All Aware and All Knowing of our best interests. Perhaps if Allah gave u that money and fame you seek it will make you transgress? Perhaps if Allah gave u that job you seek it would make you transgress? Perhaps if Allah gave you that ild you so deeply seek it would make you transgress?

I recall an incident whereby my five-year-old lost her watch after I had advised r not to wear it outside. She lost it at a park and when she informed me, I mediately scolded her as this was her Eid gift. I told her to make duah because ly Allah can help you, she silently made duah in the back of the car on the way me. Approximately a week had passed, and we went to the same park but this ne the grass had been mowed. As they were playing her brother caught a glimpse her pink watch strap lying on the grass. He screamed with glee, and she came nning besotted with joy to tell me her watch had been found and it was completely te and sound. We were in utter shock but at the same time we knew nothing is possible for Allah. We discussed how it did not rain that week and how somebody could have easily taken it, but Allah preserved it for her with and by her duah. Thus, Allah will protect you through your ad'iyah so no matter how small or big it may seem do not lose hope in asking Him continuously. Raise your hands up to Allah and let Him handle your affairs. Allah will grant you in abundance.

The perishing of this whole universe is much less for Allah then Him not fulfilling His promise to the believers. The promise of Allah is certainty, *and who is truer to his covenant than Allah?* In that case we must strengthen our faith. In the battle of Hunayn the companions depended on their large numbers to give them victory and were pleased therein. This was the reason for their downfall during this monumental battle. You must overpower your doubts and stay firm in the promise of Allah, not in your limited and weak capability. Have you realised that when you rely on yourself somehow Allah refocuses you on Him and His infinite ability? You must see the promise of Allah as true, do not ever lose trust in Allah. Allah is with the faithful servants who abide by His book and those are the ones who are victorious.

Zayd ibn Thabit reported: The Messenger of Allah, peace and blessings be upon him, said,

"Whoever makes the world his most important matter, Allah will confound his affairs and make poverty appear before his eyes and he will not get anything from the world but what has been decreed for him. Whoever makes the Hereafter his most important matter, Allah will settle his affairs and make him content in his heart and the world will come to him although he does not want it."

Sahih (authentic) according to Al-Albani.

As illustrated in this hadith, the person who makes the hereafter his main concern he will obtain three praiseworthy things

1. Allah will grant him richness and contentment of the heart.

2. Allah will rectify all his affairs; He is able to do everything with ease.

3. This world will come to him with ease.

In comparison to the one who makes this world his main concern he obtains three severe punishments

1. Allah will place poverty before his eyes; whatever of this world he has he will seek to obtain more and never reach it.

2. Allah will scatter his affairs of this world; those who have riches cannot find the time and blessing to visit umrah or do hajj, this world has busied him.

3. He will only gain from this world what is written for him, and he cannot and will not exceed it.

Therefore, whatever is written for you will not miss you. If we give great focus and precedence to the worship of Allah He will place richness in our lives and hearts. We must give time and effort to seeking knowledge and knowing our Lord. If Allah is happy with you, you will live a life of serenity. The people of the Quran recommend a daily recitation of at least five juz to finish the Quran once a week. This is a mere recitation aside from its memorization. This will bring about great blessings in abundance in your household. It will rid your home and mind of any harm and ill. It will grant your heart a tranquillity that is only found in the speech of Allah. This contentment of the heart must enter our hearts for it is a light like no other. This is also exemplified in the following narrations of the prophet,

Abu Huraira reported: The Prophet, peace and blessings be upon him, said,

"Allah Almighty said: O son of Adam, busy yourself with my worship and I will fill your heart with riches and alleviate your poverty. If you do not do so, I will fill your hands with problems and never alleviate your poverty."

Sunan al-Tirmidhī. Sahih according to Al-Albani.

Abdullah bin Amr bin Al-as (May Allah be pleased with them) reported: the Messenger of Allah (ﷺ) said,

> *"Successful is the one who has entered the fold of Islam and is provided with sustenance which is sufficient for his needs, and Allah makes him content with what He has bestowed upon him."*

Sahih Muslim.

The prophet mentioned herein three things which are connected to success.

1. Submission to the religion of Islam: the degree to which a person submits and protects his religion is in accordance to the success he is given.

2. Provision which is sufficient: without extra which leads to extravagance, that allows one to live with which suffices him of food, drink, and housing. If these are insufficient then this will cause anxiety and stress. The same if a person is given excess amounts of wealth he will be busied in that which does not concern him. Sometimes you see a man who lives a simple life and is content but if he is increased in that which he does not need he will be in a life of stress and tightness. What is the benefit in extreme amounts of wealth if it adds stress and anxiety?

3. Contentment: Allah will give him contentment in that which he is given. If he is not given contentment in his life he will be in dire distress. To be given contentment is from the treasures of Allah that does not perish. The illustrious sheikh Muhammad Al Ameen Ashinqeeti the author of the great tafseer *Adwaa Al Bayan* said to his son,

O my son I left my city of Shinqeet with a treasure that is contentment. My son, hunger is banished with a slice of bread. Not all of mankind is given contentment. The reality of this world is that it will not quench the one who seeks it ever. As for if contentment is removed from the heart, then he is a pauper.

Thus, if you are not granted contentment, you will be unsatisfied no matter how much you possess. If this world will never quench the seeker, then why must we chase it hopelessly?

His kingdom does not perish. Accordingly, when you ask Allah do not think that His dominion is reduced by giving. Do not have doubts in your duah. The ability to answer is in His control but the duah is in your control. Your voice which you think does not go beyond you goes above the seven heavens to be answered by the One who hears the call of the needy. But your heart must be present with full conviction that it will be granted. Allah does not answer the call of the absent hearted. Allah is Al Mujeeb the one who answers and responds. Allah will never forsake you. Allah saved those who were in need simply because they called onto Him. If a life is alive with the remembrance of Allah it will be energised, and his heart will be awakened. If Allah is with you who can harm you? If Allah gives you victory who can disgrace you? The remembrance of Allah is great. Ask Allah for well-being and forgiveness. The blessing of being granted good health and forgiveness are from the treasury of Allah and He can take and give to whom He wills. It was narrated that Ibn 'Umar said:

The Messenger of Allah (pbuh) never abandoned these supplications, every morning and evening: (O Allah, I ask You for forgiveness and well-being in this world and in the Hereafter. O Allah, I ask You for forgiveness and well-being in my religious and my worldly affairs. O Allah, conceal my faults, calm my fears, and protect me from before me and behind me, from my right and my left, and from above me, and I seek refuge in You from being taken unaware from beneath me).

Sahih Sunan Ibn Majah.

Ibn Qayyim said these two words *'afwa wal-'afiyah'* in it the prophet combined the affairs of this world and the hereafter. The Muslim and his uprightness in both domains exist upon these two. He said the certainty of the faith protects a person when he goes to the hereafter and the problems therein. This cannot occur except with well-being from Allah. The well-being in this life protects your body from various illness attacking your heart and body. Thus, the prophet comprised the affairs of this world in one word and the affairs of the hereafter using one word. The believer is in dire need for this supplication more so than his food and drink as his dunya and hereafter depend on their uprightness. Recite this supplication morning and evening and Allah will protect you from all problems from every direction. The great companion Abu Bakr stood on the pulpit of the prophet (pbuh) after his death and cried, he then said the prophet stood here last year and cried without speaking. Observe how closely they wanted to emulate their beloved prophet. Once he stopped crying he said 'ask Allah for forgiveness and well-being in this world'. A slave is not given anything better after Islam then forgiveness and well-being. So seek it from Him. The remembrance of Allah is like food to the heart. The heart is barren without it and cannot bear any fruits.

Death. Remember this often. The prophet advised us that death is enough as a reminder for us. Therefore, we must visit the graveyards and doing this will realign our focus in this life. If somebody is told they will die and is eating, he will not be able to finish the food he was eating. It will lose its taste. Everything will lose the value he gave it. If we remind ourselves regularly what awaits us in the lonely grave and the questioning that awaits us, you will rethink and work harder for the hereafter. If you observe the people in the graves and how long they have been inside and the varying ages this enough will awake you. You must prepare for this whilst you have the chance. There are many events awaiting the human in front of Allah and the destination is paradise or hellfire.

And the Horn will be blown, and whoever is in the heavens and whoever is on the earth will fall dead except whom Allah wills. Then it will be blown again, and at once they will be standing, looking on.

Surah Zumar: Verse 68.

Allah tells us about the terrors of that day. On that day his good deeds will be with him. What will aid you in remembering Allah and the hereafter often is having the remembrance of Allah on your tongue and holding tightly to them. This is the Quran and the legislated athkar. You must hold tightly on to these. The more you increase in His remembrance the more you will be beloved to Allah. If you are beloved to Allah nothing and nobody else matters.

Sometimes Allah wants to redirect you back to Him and remind you that he is the ally for all your affairs. From Allah's beautiful names and attributes is the name

28

l-Mudabbir – The Ruler, the Director who governs all the creation with great order
nd balance. In the story of Musa alayhi salam as we mentioned previously, Pharoah
ssued to kill baby boys one year and pardon them the other. Musa was destined to
e born the year the order of the killings was issued. When Umm Musa gave birth,
he was fearful for her baby, but Allah gave her a Lordly inspiration not to fear and
nat her son would be returned to her. At this moment she was granted firmness in
er reliance to Him. Where is the tadbeer of Allah? In the very house of Pharoah.
ne wife of Pharoah did not have children but Allah instilled in her an excessive
ve for baby Musa from the minute she laid eyes on him. Who is the one who gave
is victory? Allah. Sometimes Allah directs and governs your affairs whilst you walk
out your life and do not see. For example, your sustenance that you live off daily.
llah protects your provision for you until it comes directly to you. There is a story
f a man who was trapped inside a well for a long time. He was rescued and brought
ck up to safety, he was given a cup of milk and people began to question what had
ppened to him. Whilst he was retelling the sequence of events he fell back into
e same well and died instantly. What was left from his sustenance that was
eordained was that glass of milk. He was not meant to die until he drank from that
p.

Allah is the One who is ordering and controlling all your affairs for you. Allah is
e Director of your life. Not you. We must have firm reliance upon Him. Firstly,
e must pay close attention to our relationship with Allah. Secondly, we must always
se our hands to Allah and say O Allah direct my life for me, O Allah make me
essed wherever You may place me. O Allah grant me Your love. By Allah, if Allah
ants you this goodness you will see amazement in all the affairs of your life, in your
stenance and in your household. Allah will rectify the affairs between you and the
ople. If you rectify that which is between you and Allah, He will rectify the affairs
tween you and everybody else. If you fear Allah, He will grant you ease and a way
t. This is a principle if you fear Him, He will grant you an exit. So have glad tidings
goodness awaiting you for verily Allah is Subtle and Kind to His servants.

Growth

Sometimes you must enter a door regardless of how painful it is, you may even be sitting with your back to it. You may have bolted the door shut in a bid to avoid opening it. If it is destined for you, you must enter through it. Because through that door lies therein your freedom. This first step will open many other doors for you. Opportunities you never thought were possible and only dreamed of. You must take that first step and open the door with good thoughts from a Lord who is generous and giving.

Do not hang on to somebody who already let go of you. Have some compassion for yourself! Do what you must to take care of yourself and don't you dare feel guilty. Instead of always sacrificing and investing in others invest in yourself. Do not let people stay in your mind rent free. Unless they are paying rent of which its currency is peace, support, empathy, love and prioritising your needs. Evict them and their toxicity. Granting some people your energy is akin to handing them the bullets to shoot you with. Do not base your worth on them. These are individuals who are unaware of their own self and carry excess baggage they refuse to claim. Before the truth can free them, they must recognize which lie has imprisoned and shackled them. Free yourself from that which does not serve you. There are so many walking people who appear to be whole, but they are entirely broken and search for healing in all the wrong places.

The way people treat you reflects more about them than you. It is not upon you to take the burden of the people and what they say about you. The same people that oppress you are the very people that Allah will recompense. In this world before the hereafter. The same people who put you down and abuse you are the ones who see something great within you that they do not and never will possess. Reawaken what you lost and search for what you always had. Reclaim your sense of self. The same people that brought you pain stalk you to check if you are happy without them. This is an emotion they are incapable of having but little do they know that the trash finally took itself out.

Is he, then, to whom the evil of his deeds is made fairseeming, so that he considers it as good Verily, Allah sends astray whom He wills, and guides whom He wills. So destroy not yourself in sorrow for them. Truly, Allah is the All-Knower of what they do!

Surah Fatir: Verse 8.

This ayah provides consolation in the fact that the previous Messengers were denied, yet there is also a stark reminder to the one whose evil deeds **appear** to be good. You see our religion does not place value on appearance. It is the intention that is pivotal. These types of people think they are collecting many good deeds. However, the heart is corrupt. Who is the one who has beautified their evil actions for them? Shaytaan has done so making them fair seeming. If your actions are not done for the sake of Allah and following the messenger (s.a.w's) path it will be null and void. Towards the end of the ayah Allah gives great comfort by telling us not to throw ourselves into sorrow over them. Almost as if they are meaningless and all they seek is the apparent, but they are hollow and empty internally. Allah reminds us that He is all aware of what they do. Correct your heart and the path you follow; this rectification will carry your deeds for you far and beyond your capability. As for those that are corrupt and seek people's pleasure Allah will always reveal their true intention although they may be seemingly pleasant.

If your feet ache it is because you are a traveller on this path. The prophet was called a magician, a liar, a madman, and he died although he was the leader of the first and last. Allah will be your ally for all your affairs. Musa was harmed by his own people and what they said about him. Until he cut off from them and he would bathe alone, yet even then they did not leave him. They persisted and followed him until they said he had a defect in him which is the reason he hid away. They insulted him with something he was free from. Have conviction in Allah for verily He is the best ally you could ever have, if you have Allah what have you lost?

Everything in this world points to the certainty of Allah's existence. He may put you in certain situations to bring you closer to Him. Likewise, He may take you out of situations to draw you nearer to Him. Have certainty in His plan and His divine decree. Be happy with certainty. The truth will prevail, and falsehood will always perish. Hold onto the non-perishing threshold of Allah. Have certainty in His promise. For verily Allah will never forsake you. Beware of becoming weak or scared. For verily Allah is the ally for the affairs of His servants. This entire universe is by and at the order of Allah. He is the turner of hearts.

When women put make up on our beauty is exemplified more then we began with. But what if the same woman ate the same make-up she put on? It would most likely put her in hospital, and she may even die of poisoning. Thus, when everything is placed in other then its rightful position it can bring about great harm. For this reason, this position in your life and stage you are at is with a Lordly wisdom. Your destiny was decreed thousands of years before you. If you live with this notion your mind-frame, existence, patience, and ability will be beautified. The trial you are in will be lessened. You must go forth with all your ability and do all you can without falling short. Allah wants to cleanse and purify you. The most sought-after possessions in this world for beauty, a time came about whereby it had no value nor could people stand it. For example, diamonds are only found in a select number of countries hundreds of miles deep underground. Only after enduring the process of rough mining, heat, pressure, and deep cleansing is it placed in a protective place with security behind mirrors holding the highest value. I promise you; your beauty is what will surface from this trial. I promise you; you must value and guard this with the highest of esteem and security.

You are special. You are bold. You are strong. You are beautiful. You are resilient. You are loved. You are worthy. You are unique. You are worthy. Allah created you to be different. Allah made you, you. He fashioned you to be incredible. Do not believe people's negative opinions of you. It usually reflects more about them then you. People deflect and project their insecurities onto others in a bid to feel superior.

You are reading this for a reason. You are in this very moment with me for a reason. You must convince your heart that the decree of Allah is good for you always. You are right where you should and need to be. Whatever He decreed is the most beneficial and appropriate for you. Put your trust in Allah and keep moving forward. A Lord that loves you more than your mother will always put your best interest first. If you are patient Allah will purify you of your sins. Sometimes, Allah delays the relief for a greater reason. But we as humans become tired and hastily want it to end. If Allah delays the relief know that He wants you to meet Him without any sins. How loving He is. Allah knows we are weak and collect sins upon sins, so He wants to purify us so that we meet Him cleansed and purified. A loving Lord.

Whatever you focus on will grow. You must minimize the disease of overthinking aspects of your life. Do not ask yourself when you will surpass this test, hand your affairs over to Allah. The human beings strongest change and growth comes around more often when he is going through a difficult time. This is the stage in your life that will change and uplift you to a higher level. If you see every trial as a means for you to excel, your mind frame and what you focus on will change. Where you stand today is a proof that you will move on from whatever it is that is on your mind so heavily. What is to come is better than what has passed. You can rise from anything and completely recreate yourself you are not stuck anywhere. You are not a tree. Move. You can create new habits and all that matters is that you decide today and never look back. Breath, darling. This is just a chapter in your life it is not the whole story.

A day will come where you will become somebody with a higher being and better life. This second will pass and do not estimate your future with your current situation. Make your tongue moist with the remembrance of Allah. In every situation seek Allah and make supplication to Him. Allah is not unaware He can change your situation with ease but where is your input? Perhaps this trial was sent to you because you became forgetful of Allah for a time, so He wants to hear your call and rectify this life and your hereafter in the best of ways. Run to Allah. Go to Allah with your weakness and you will return with strength from Him. This is the happiness of this world, to be able to hand your affairs to Allah who is all able and all capable. Subsequently, if you go to mankind at the most you will receive some pity. Allah is the One who answers the needy one and you have a Lord who is shy to return you empty handed.

Life transforming beliefs are found in the most diverse of moments this is a fact and when you make that your mindset it will transform you. Allah is with the wronged. If a calamity or a trial befalls you search for the blessing behind it, and you will find it. Similarly, if a blessing befalls you search for the trial behind it, and you will find it. Every hardship has with it, blessings so search for it and then you will taste its sweetness. A calamity afflicts the servant of Allah but when he knows that this is from Allah his heart is content. Accordingly, Allah ascribed to Himself that He is the most Merciful the most Forgiving. Everything you have been blessed with search behind it the test, beware of it wherever it may be, whoever it may be, whatever it may be.

You are going to realise it one day – that happiness was never about your status or being with the right person. Happiness was never about people and making them happy. Happiness was never about accumulating wealth. True happiness lies in knowing Allah and seeking a life to please Him. One day, you will understand that happiness was about learning how to live and be content within yourself. It was never in the hands of others. It should have never been placed in their hands. You must let go of the picture of what you thought your life would be like and learn to find happiness in the story you are actually in. Put the spotlight on the page you are on in your life now. They are all imperfectly perfect. Trust Allah. It was always about you. It was you all along. It was you.

Sis, the next chapter of your life is called growth. Tiers of growth. He will break you to make you whole again. Until the pain becomes sweet you will not forgo the ial you are in. Until you are thankful for the trials sent your way to build you, they ill be sent again and again. Until it is a joy to you the test will remain. Until you are nankful for it being sent your way to build you, they will be sent again and again. llah is building you for resilience to go onto something greater. Your trials are tailor ade for you. To you. You cannot go through the test somebody else may be given. ikewise, they cannot go through your test. It was uniquely chosen for you. So much), that you will look back and not be able to recognise the woman you left behind. /ho was she? I hear you say. This is what growth looks like and I must say it looks od on you.

Printed in Great Britain
by Amazon

65887550R00024